A TASTE OF CHINA

Roz Denny

Thomson Learning
New York

Titles in this series

Britain	Italy
China	Japan
France	Mexico
India	West Africa

Cover background: *Southern China is known for its spectacular hill scenery. In front of the hills are rice paddies.*
Foreground: *Children from the Ge minority, in traditional dress, eating rice.*

Frontispiece: *A young girl using chopsticks to eat noodles. Noodles and rice form an important part of the Chinese diet.*

First published in the
United States in 1994 by
Thomson Learning
115 Fifth Avenue
New York, NY 10003

First published in Great Britain in 1994 by
Wayland (Publishers) Ltd.

UK version copyright © 1994 Wayland
(Publishers) Ltd.

U.S. version copyright © 1994 Thomson Learning

Library of Congress Cataloging-in-Publication Data
Denny, Roz.
A taste of China / Roz Denny.
p.   cm. —(Food around the world)
Includes bibliographical references (p. 47) and index.
ISBN 1-56847-183-1
1. Cookery, China—Juvenile literature. 2. Food habits—China—
Juvenile literature. 3. China—Social life and customs.
[1. Cookery, Chinese. 2. Food habits—China.
3. China—Social life and customs.]
I. Series.
TX724.5.C5D42   1994
641.5951—dc20   94-734

Printed in Italy

Contents

"The middle of the world"

China is a very crowded country. In the evenings, city streets are full of people cycling home from work.

China is the third largest country in the world and has the greatest population. It has over one billion people – about one-fifth of the world's population.

Chinese civilization goes back 5,000 years. Even before the great civilizations of ancient Greece and Rome, Chinese people were skilled in the arts, mathematics, and music. Many Chinese thought people who lived to the west of their country were wild barbarians and, until the last hundred years or so, wished to have little to do with them. As a result, China has remained quite a mystery to people in the West.

In the West, people think of China as being part of the Far East (it is situated on the eastern side of the vast continent of Asia). The Chinese, however, think of themselves as being in the middle of the world. They call their country "*Zhongguo,*" which means "middle of the world." The name China dates from the third century B.C., when the country was ruled by emperors of the Qin (pronounced "chin") dynasty.

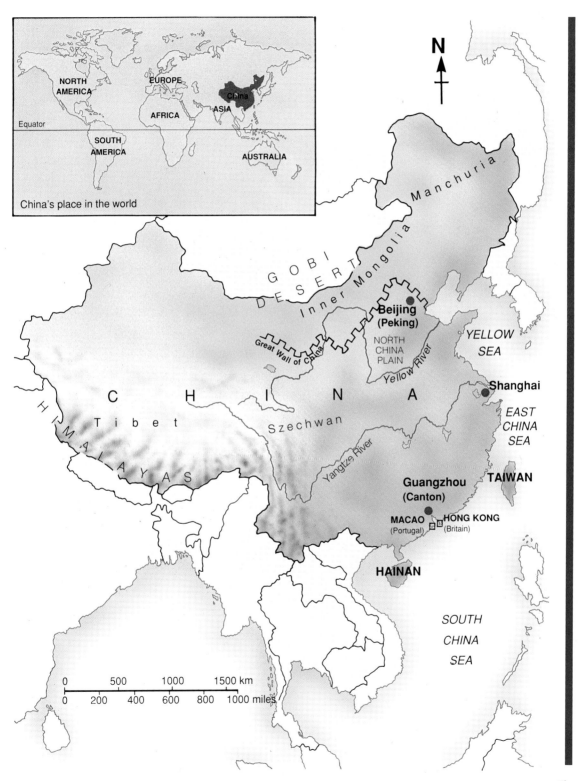

China's place in the world

For thousands of years, the Chinese kept themselves apart from the rest of the world. More than 2,000 years ago, they built the Great Wall of China to keep out invaders.

Over the centuries, the strongest link there has been between China and the West is probably China's food. There are many different styles of Chinese food. China is an enormous country with great differences in weather and landscape, so the foods that can be grown vary greatly from region to region. In the north and west the food can be hot and spicy. In the south the food is lighter and includes many things unusual to Western peoples.

In the nineteenth century, many Chinese traveled abroad to work as laborers or traders. Many set up restaurants and food stores. In this way, delicious Chinese dishes have been introduced in many countries. Stir-fries, spareribs, spring rolls, and fried rice have become popular around the world.

Chinese people living in other countries also adapted their recipes to suit local foods. For example, one so-called Chinese dish, chop suey, does not come from China at all, but from the west coast of the United States.

In the nineteenth century, many Chinese left to live in other parts of the world. This is Chinatown in San Francisco. It is an interesting mix of Chinese and American traditions.

China today

In this book, we shall look only at mainland China, although there are a number of Chinese outposts. The island of Taiwan is ruled by its own Western-style government. Hong Kong is a group of islands governed by Britain. In 1997 it is due to become part of China again.

The China of today is very different from that of forty to fifty years ago. China is a Communist country. Communists believe that everyone is equal and that no one should own property or have more possessions than anyone else. So all land and buildings belong to the state. In other words, all the people in China own the land and buildings collectively, or all together, and each person must work for the good of the community.

This attitude has had a great effect on farming, industry, and trade. Some people believe that it has greatly improved the lives of most Chinese people. Until 1949, when the Communists took control of the government, millions of Chinese

The Communist leader, Mao Tse-tung, set up the modern People's Republic of China in 1949, bringing enormous changes to the country. He died in 1976. There are many statues of him.

7

peasants suffered great hardship from bad crops, poor farming methods, bad weather, and cruel property owners. Floods and droughts often led to famines, which killed millions of people. Today, food supplies, health, and education are much better and there are no longer terrible famines.

Although China has several big cities, most people live in the countryside. Living conditions remain simple. Houses usually have only one floor and are often built around a courtyard, with kitchens and bathrooms shared among a number of families. Water may be taken from a village well, although water

Above *The Chinese capital, Beijing, is a big, modern city, but old buildings have been preserved.* Below *Country life: houses built around a shared courtyard.*

Right *In many villages, people fetch water from a shared well.*

pipes are now being connected to some homes. Usually, grandparents, parents, and children live together. Most women work, so the grandparents take care of the children.

The Chinese population is rapidly growing larger than its resources can support. To deal with this problem, the government is trying to persuade married couples to have only one child. However, there are still families with several children.

More than 90 percent of the people are Han Chinese – the original Chinese – but there are also many minority races. These include the Zhuang, the Tibetans, and many others.

Above *A government wall painting encouraging one-child families.*
Below *Women from the Tuzu minority, in traditional clothes.*

Landscape and climate

Above *Much of northwest China is cold and dry. Few plants can grow.*

Four-fifths of China is covered by mountains, swamp, or desert, making it unsuitable for growing crops. As a result, the remaining fifth of the land, which is good for farming, is used to produce as much food as possible.

China has a great variety of climates and landscapes. The north is dry and barren. Here lies the Gobi Desert, where the weather can get very cold in winter. In the west are the icy Himalayan Mountains, while in the south, around Guangzhou (Canton), it is hot and semitropical. In the east are flat, fertile plains.

Most of China, in fact, has a temperate climate. This means it is not too hot and not too cold, with moderate amounts of rainfall. However, the south is affected by monsoon winds and rains from the Pacific Ocean. Heavy monsoon rains can cause terrible flooding, killing people, animals, and crops.

Left *The hot, wet weather of southern China produces lush, green scenery.*

Yellow loess scenery. Much of the soil has been worn away, leaving a bare, rugged landscape.

During the winter, icy winds sweep down from Siberia. As they blow over the Gobi Desert the winds pick up a fine yellow dust, which they later drop farther to the south and east. This fine dust becomes a fertile soil called loess. However, it is easily washed away in floods. Much of it is swept onto the North China Plain by the Yellow River.

China is a land of rivers. The main ones are the Yangtze River and the Yellow River. Until recent years the Yellow River often flooded. Crops were ruined and there was death and destruction. The Communist government has introduced modern methods to try to control the flooding and improve irrigation for crops.

A water control station on a canal near the Yellow River.

Farming and crops

Working in the fields. Today, people have a piece of land on which to grow their own vegetables.

In China, farms are not owned by one person or company, as they usually are in the West. All the land is owned by the state. In the past, people were encouraged to form groups, working together to produce crops for everyone. More recently, people have been allowed

to farm for their own profit. Some of the produce goes to the state, but the people are allowed to sell the rest. In addition, people are now allowed to work a small plot of land on which to grow their own vegetables, which they can either sell in the market or eat themselves.

Nearly two-thirds of the population works on the land. Because so little land is suitable for growing crops, farmers have to grow as much as possible on the land available. This is called intensive farming. Much of the work is done by hand or using simple tools, although more modern machinery is now being introduced.

People sell any spare vegetables at market.

An ox and simple plow being used to prepare a rice field.

Wheat is an important crop in northern China. Here, the grains are being separated from the stalks by throwing the cut wheat into the air.

Young rice plants are planted out in flooded fields called paddies. Rice needs plenty of water to grow. The water also protects the plants from being eaten by insects.

The main crops grown are wheat, millet, and soybeans in the north; corn in the center; and rice in the south. In the far south of China the climate is mild enough to grow two crops of rice a year. This is very useful with so many millions of mouths to feed. Tea is

another important crop, and it is grown around the Yangtze River.

The Chinese have always been good at making the most of what they have. With irrigation and the use of natural fertilizers, they are able to keep the land rich in nutrients. Hills are often terraced – small, flat fields are cut into the sides. This means that rice can be grown in paddies, which are flooded with water. The water is held in place by stone walls.

China has little spare land for animals to graze on, so people raise pigs, chickens, or ducks. These animals do not need grass and take up little space. In the north and west of the country, there is grazing land where people raise yaks (a kind of cattle) and sheep.

Looking down on a neatly terraced hillside. By cutting terraces, farmers create more land for growing crops.

Yaks grazing in Tibet. They are a type of long-haired cattle.

15

The food regions of China

The basic foods of China are the same throughout the country, and the cooking methods are similar. Variations in cooking styles come from the ingredients used. Chinese food writers say there are four main food regions.

Northern cuisine
The northern style of cooking is centered around the capital, Beijing (Peking), and includes Mongolian and Manchurian dishes. Here, wheat is the main crop and it is made into noodles, steamed bread, or dumplings.

Noodles are sold fresh or dried. These have been hung up to dry.

To eat Peking duck, each person makes his or her own parcels of crisp meat, wrapped in thin pancakes, with vegetables and sauce.

A famous dish is Peking duck. The duck is marinated and roasted until crisp by hanging it in an oven. It is then carved, and the pieces of meat are wrapped in thin pancakes, with shredded cucumber and scallions and a sweet plum sauce.

Mongolian hot pot

This is a warming dish for the cold Mongolian climate. A large pot containing hot stock is placed in the center of the table, over burning coals. Each diner picks up thin cut pieces of raw food, such as lamb, liver, and vegetables, with chopsticks and pops them into the simmering stock. The food takes just seconds to cook and is then taken out and eaten. At the end of the meal the stock has become a delicious soup, which is ladled into bowls and drunk.

A taste of China

Chinese vegetables. Bamboo shoots (center) are very popular. This picture also shows ginger, scallions, fresh coriander, tomatoes.

Fresh fish for sale in Shanghai.

Eastern cuisine

This is centered around the seaport of Shanghai. The food is rich, sweet, and contains a lot of fat and oil. This is a very fertile part of China where excellent vegetables are grown. There is also a long coastline bordering the East China Sea and the Pacific Ocean. Here the Yangtze River empties into the sea and there are plenty of fish and shellfish – both freshwater and saltwater.

A speciality from this region is a technique called "red cooking." Food is cooked slowly in dark soy sauce, giving it a reddish color.

Southern or Cantonese cuisine

This is perhaps the best-known food outside China, as many people from Guangzhou (called Canton in English) left China to live in the West. Ingredients unusual in the West are used, such as snakes, turtles, sea urchins, sharks' fins, and even rice worms (the Chinese are very adventurous and are happy to try most foods).

Cantonese cooking is light in style, using a blend of sauces, such as soy sauce and oyster sauce (see page 23), with oils made from crushed sesame seeds. Food is lightly cooked by steaming or stir-frying. Famous Cantonese dishes include sweet and sour pork, dim sum, and wontons, which are small filled dumplings served floating in soup.

Wontons are soft dumplings filled with meat and spices.

Dim sum

Dim sum (pictured) are bite-sized snacks eaten as a quick, light meal and served with tea. In dim sum restaurants, waiters and waitresses walk between the tables, pushing carts that are piled high with steamed and fried dumplings, fried crispy rolls, or little croquettes, all arranged prettily in small bamboo baskets. Diners simply take their pick.

Dried mushrooms on sale in Yunnan Province.

Western cuisine, or Szechwan

Food from the provinces of Szechwan and Hunan is generally hot and spicy. The main flavorings used are ginger, garlic, red chili peppers, and little, aromatic red peppercorns. Two well-known dishes from this area are hot and sour soup and fragrant crispy duck.

Another province in this part of China, called Yunnan, produces a special type of ham and a great variety of mushrooms – as many as 250.

Cooking the Chinese way

Chinese cooking is very simple. It helps to have all the food prepared and chopped first. Then the cooking takes next to no time.

There are four main cooking methods: stir-frying, steaming, slow cooking or braising, and deep-frying. These methods of cooking developed because, until recently, China was short of slow-burning fuels, such as coal or gas. So quick cooking methods were developed using wood or charcoal fires.

A wok and wok scoop are essential pieces of cooking equipment. The wok has a rounded bottom.

Cooking utensils

The main cooking pot is called a wok. This is a large, bowl-shaped frying pan. The rounded shape of the wok lets the heat spread evenly all over the pan. The deep sides make stirring and tossing the food easy.

A wok can also be used as a steamer, by placing bamboo baskets inside it. And it can be used for deep-frying, too, by filling it one-third full with oil.

To chop vegetables, meat, and fish, Chinese cooks use a very sharp cleaver.

21

A taste of China

A large cleaver is used for chopping. Chinese cooks are skilled at cutting meat and vegetables into very small pieces.

Bamboo steamers are used to cook dumplings. Here, steam is rising from the top.

Turned on its side, the cleaver can also be used to beat tough pieces of meat to make them tender. Chopping boards are round, because normally they are simply a slice from a large tree.

To steam food, the Chinese use bamboo baskets with lids. These fit inside a wok with a little water in the base. The wok is covered with a large, domed lid. Bamboo steamers are made to stack on top of one another.

To stir, toss, or drain food, the Chinese use long chopsticks, wok scoops, and bamboo-handled strainers.

And that is basically it!

Food preparation

For quick stir-frying, all pieces of food are cut to the same size. Foods that take longer to cook are put into the wok first. Other foods are added later, according to how much cooking time they need. Any flavorings and sauces are mixed together in a cup or bowl, then stirred in at the end.

Sometimes, pieces of food are marinated in soy sauce, garlic, or ginger before cooking. This adds extra flavor. Another common cooking technique, used for meat or fish, is to precook foods slowly, by steaming or braising, until they are tender. Then they are drained, patted dry, and quickly deep-fried until crisp.

Stir-frying in a wok. A scoop is used to toss and stir the pieces of food.

Chinese flavorings

The Chinese like to use many spices and sauces in their cooking. Few foods, except perhaps rice, are served unflavored. These are the main flavorings used.

Soy sauce This dark, salty liquid is used in most dishes. It is made from fermented soybeans, with wheat, salt, sugar, and yeast. There are two main types – dark and light.

Oyster sauce Similar to soy sauce but made from oysters. It is milder and slightly sweeter than soy sauce.

Sesame oil A light-brown, very aromatic oil made by pressing roasted sesame seeds. It is used for flavoring more than for frying.

Ginger root The light-brown root of the ginger plant, which is peeled and grated. It is quite hot and spicy.

A taste of China

Five spice powder A mixture of five spices: star anise, cinnamon, coriander, cloves, and fennel seeds. It is strong, so only a little is used at a time.

Rice wine This is used in sauces mixed with soy sauce and sesame oil. Dry sherry can be used instead.

Worcestershire sauce This is a British sauce, similar to soy sauce, which the Chinese now use in great quantity.

Garlic A strong-tasting bulb similar to an onion.

Chilies Red and green chili peppers are used to add a spicy "hotness" to dishes. Chilies are very popular in Szechwan cooking.

Dried spices are sold whole or ground to a powder for cooking. The brown bark (top left) is cinnamon; the red pods (top right) are chilies; the brown stars (center) are star anise.

A woman preparing chili peppers.

How a Chinese meal is put together

A Chinese meal consists of two parts. The main core of the meal is called *fan*. This is a grain-based food such as boiled or steamed rice, noodles (made from wheat), or steamed wheat buns. *Fan* is accompanied by at least two other dishes, called *cai*. These are vegetable or meat dishes. Everyone has his or her own bowl of rice or other *fan*, but the *cai* dishes are put in the center of the table for everyone to share. The people at the table use their chopsticks to help themselves to what they want. Traditionally, wealthy families had more than two *cai* dishes and for special celebrations even more. Soup is served in small bowls with spoons, either between courses or at the end of a meal. Usually, there is no dessert, although some fresh fruit may be eaten.

Chinese families like to eat together. Good manners are considered very important. Guests are offered the best pieces of food and the conversation at the table will generally be about the cooking.

The evening meal: a boy helps himself from a selection of cai *dishes.*

A taste of China

The symbol for Yin and Yang gives an impression of perfect balance. It is sometimes used on jewelry.

Yin and Yang

There are a number of ancient Chinese philosophies that the Chinese apply to food and health. The main one is Yin and Yang. According to this system, all foods belong to one of three groups. Yin are cooling foods, Yang are heating foods, and Yin Yang are those in the middle, such as bread and rice. The Chinese classify people in the same way. A Yin person is quiet; a Yang person is outgoing.

To create a perfectly balanced and therefore healthy meal, the Chinese believe these three elements must be blended together. Chinese recipes place great importance on the blending of flavors – sweet and sour, for example, or hot and sour. At a full meal, one dish will be hot, another mild or crispy.

Chinese seven tastes

In the West people recognize four main tastes – salty, sweet, sour, and bitter. The Chinese include three more: hot or fiery; an oniony, garlicky flavor that they call *xiang*; and the seventh taste, called *xian*, meaning "delicious" (this includes tomatoes, mushrooms, and any extra flavor sprinkled on food just before it is served).

Everyday eating and drinking

The Chinese eat three meals a day. The midday and evening meals are much the same, both consisting of *fan* and a number of *cai*.

Breakfast foods differ from north to south. In the north, breakfast is usually a steamed wheat bun stuffed with pickles, accompanied by soy milk (the Chinese do not care for cow's milk). In the south, a piping-hot porridge made of rice, called *congee*, is eaten. This is accompanied by pickled turnip or cabbage, perhaps with ham or sausage. Tea is not drunk at breakfast. This is more a Western habit.

Many people who live in towns and cities pick up breakfast on their way to work. They buy big bowls of hot soy milk and long, twisted sticks of savory dough, which are deep-fried like our doughnuts.

For children, lunch at school is generally a bowl of rice with one or two accompanying dishes. These may be vegetables, soybean curd (tofu), and perhaps some meat or fish.

Breakfast at a street stall on the way to school and work. This family is eating soup and dough sticks.

A taste of China

Many young children spend the day at a nursery set up at the office or factory where their parents work. The nursery provides lunch.

Sweet desserts are not served at mealtimes but are bought as treats from stores. A kind of ice cream is popular. This is more like our water ice and is not made from milk. There are also sweet, steamed buns filled with soybean paste.

Eating with chopsticks

The Chinese have used thin, wooden chopsticks for thousands of years. They use them for both cooking and eating. Here are some hints on using chopsticks.

1 Clasp your thumb and last three fingers together, with your index finger up in the air.

2 Place one chopstick along your straightened middle finger and against the base of your thumb, holding it firmly with your middle finger. Place the other chopstick on top, holding it between your index finger and the top of your thumb.

3 Now you can move the top chopstick up and down while holding the bottom one still. Practice picking up small items. You will soon get the hang of it.

Eating rice

It is considered polite to hold a small bowl of rice up to your mouth and to scoop the rice in using chopsticks. If you pick up food from the center of the table, place it in your bowl of rice first before eating it. Do not put it straight into your mouth – this is considered bad manners.

Holding chopsticks correctly.

When eating rice, it is usual to hold the bowl up to your mouth and scoop in the rice with chopsticks.

29

A taste of China

Tea plants are leafy bushes. They are grown on plantations in close rows. When ready, the leaves are picked by hand.

At tea houses, people stop for a refreshing drink and a chat with friends.

Tea in China

The Chinese were the first people to discover a drink made from tea. People drink tea throughout a meal, not just at the end. It is very weak, and no milk or sugar is added. It is served in small, handleless cups.

There are three main types of tea. Green tea is made by simply drying the fresh tea leaves. This produces a pale yellow drink with a slightly sharp flavor. Black tea is made by fermenting the green leaves until they become black and develop a stronger flavor. This is the type of tea drunk in the West. In fact, many Chinese dislike black tea. Another kind of tea is made by partly fermenting the leaves. This is called *oolong* tea.

It would be wrong to suggest, though, that Chinese people drink tea all the time. In fact, at meals, they are more likely to have thin, clear soup as a refreshing drink.

Festival food

From time to time, the Communist government has tried to discourage festivals, describing them as "wasteful." However, the Chinese love to celebrate – and to eat – and they have a number of festivals during the year. The main one is the Chinese New Year. This takes place between the end of January and middle of February. The exact date varies because it depends on the time of the new moon.

The New Year's festival can last for up to two weeks. It is a time for all the

Chinese New Year is a colorful occasion. Folk dancers with painted faces perform in the streets.

family to gather together to share food and to toast one another with tea or rice wine. There are special sweet treats: *nian gao* is a round, sticky cake made with rice flour; eight treasure rice is a pudding made with rice, red dates, red bean paste, and lotus seeds. Other special foods include wheat dumplings stuffed with vegetables, called *jiaozi*. As in all Chinese festivals, banners and paper decorations are put up, there are dancers and singers in the streets, and in the evenings fireworks are set off.

Another popular festival is the Moon festival, which takes place in the autumn. People sit out at night to look at the moon and eat moon cakes. These are round, baked cakes filled with sweet fillings made of lotus seeds, dates, or almonds. People also eat moon-shaped fruits such as melons and peaches.

This man is making moon cakes for the Moon festival. This is a time when people eat moon-shaped foods.

Five-spice spareribs

Five spice is a strong-flavored mixture of cinnamon, star anise, coriander, cloves, and fennel seeds. Together with soy sauce and sesame oil it adds a very typical, Chinese flavor to spareribs.

Ingredients
Serves 4–6

2 tablespoons light soy sauce

1 tablespoon wine vinegar

1 teaspoon sesame oil

1 tablespoon clear honey

1 teaspoon five spice

1 clove garlic

small piece of fresh root ginger, the size of a walnut

2 lb. short spareribs, pork or lamb

Spicy spareribs are brown and glossy.

33

A taste of China

Equipment

measuring spoons
cup
large plastic food bag
  and twist tie
garlic press
grater
roasting pan
aluminum foil
wooden spoon
oven mitts
kitchen tongs
serving plate

2   Peel the garlic and crush it in a garlic press. Peel and grate the ginger. Put these into the food bag too and mix well together.

3   Add the spareribs and rub the mixture into the meat. Tie the top of the bag with a twist tie and refrigerate for 4 to 8 hours, turning and rubbing the bag once or twice during this time.

1   Mix the soy sauce, vinegar, sesame oil, honey, and five spice together in a cup and pour into a large food bag.

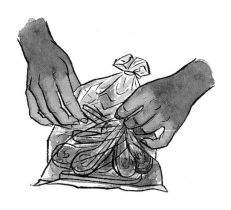

4 Preheat the oven to 325°F. Turn the ribs and the spicy mixture out into the roasting pan. Cover with a sheet of aluminum foil.

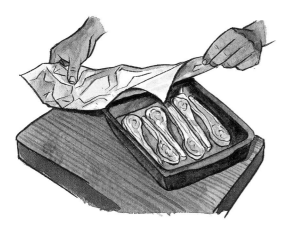

Always be careful with a hot oven. Wear oven gloves. Ask an adult to help you.

6 Turn the oven up to 400°F. Take the foil off the pan and return the pan to the oven, until the ribs turn brown and glossy. This will take about 20 minutes. You should stir them at least once in this time.

5 Cook the ribs for about 1 hour. Once or twice during this cooking time, take the pan out of the oven (wear oven mitts) and stir the spareribs around with a wooden spoon.

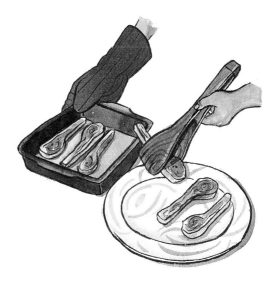

7 Carefully remove the pan from the oven. Pick the ribs up with kitchen tongs and put them on a serving plate.

Chinese tea eggs with dipping salt

Ingredients
Serves 4

4 small eggs
2 tablespoons
   Lapsang Souchong
   or Earl Grey tea
   leaves
2½ cups boiling water
2 tablespoons soy
   sauce
1 tablespoon fine sea
   salt
1 tablespoon red or
   black peppercorns
bok choy

Equipment

small saucepan
tablespoon
teakettle
pitcher
tea strainer
knife
serving plate
small dish
pepper mill

These look really pretty laid out on bok choy leaves (a pale green salad vegetable available from supermarkets and grocery stores). You can buy red peppercorns from a Chinese food store; otherwise, use black pepper. The idea is that people pick up a quarter of egg in their fingers, dip it into the spicy salt, and eat it.

Tea eggs have an unusual marbled white.

Always be careful with boiling liquid. Ask an adult to help you.

1 Carefully put the eggs in a saucepan, cover with cold water, and bring to a boil. Boil the eggs for 8 minutes.

2 Remove the pan from the heat and carefully drain the water into the sink. Stand the pan under the faucet and run cold water over the eggs for about 3 minutes. Let the eggs cool in cold water for 10 minutes, then drain.

3 Tap the eggshells on a hard surface until they are cracked all over. Do *not* peel.

4 Make the tea in a pitcher with the tea leaves and the 2½ cups boiling water. Strain it into the saucepan. Add the soy sauce.

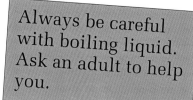

5 Put the eggs into the tea, bring to a boil, and simmer for 10 minutes. Remove from the heat and allow to sit in the water for another 15 minutes. Drain and, when cool, carefully peel off the shells. Underneath, the egg whites should have a pretty marbled pattern on them.

6 Cut the eggs in quarters, lengthwise. Arrange in a circle on a serving plate lined with bok choy leaves.

7 Put the salt in a small dish. Put the peppercorns in an empty peppermill and grind on top of the salt. Mix the salt and pepper lightly together. Put the dish in the center of the serving plate.

Egg drop soup

Ingredients
Serves 4

1 quart stock, either chicken or vegetable
2 tablespoons light soy sauce
2 scallions, peeled
a large handful of lettuce or spinach or watercress leaves, washed
2 eggs
1 teaspoon sesame oil
salt and ground black pepper

Equipment

saucepan
knife and chopping board
measuring cup
small bowl or pitcher
whisk
wooden spoon
long chopsticks or long-handled fork
4 soup bowls

This soup can be made in minutes. If you do not have any homemade stock or canned broth, use a bouillon cube mixed in boiling water. The eggs set almost instantly into pretty strands as they are stirred into the hot soup; they look like frilly flowers.

Egg drop soup is also called egg flower soup, because of the frilly strands of egg.

Always be careful with knives and hot liquid. Ask an adult to help you.

1   Put the stock and soy sauce in a saucepan and heat gently.

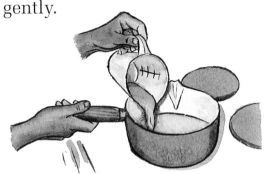

2   Chop the scallions into very thin rings. Shred the lettuce, spinach, or watercress leaves into long strands with a knife on a chopping board.

3   Break the eggs into the pitcher and beat them well. Add some salt and pepper.

4   Put the scallions and shredded leaves into the hot stock. Stir until the leaves wilt. Then bring the soup to a medium boil. Stir in the sesame oil.

5   Pour the eggs into the soup in a thin, steady stream. Count to five, then stir the soup briskly with chopsticks or a long fork. The egg will set into long, frilly strands.

6   Serve in warmed bowls.

Stir-fried chicken with peanuts

The secret of stir-frying is to get all the ingredients chopped and ready first. Make sure they are all chopped to an even size. Lay out the ingredients on small saucers and mix the sauce ingredients together in a cup. You will find it then takes only minutes to cook.

Ingredients

Serves 4

½ lb. boneless, skinless chicken breast
3 scallions
1 small red or yellow pepper
1 clove garlic
small piece of fresh ginger root, the size of a walnut
2 tablespoons vegetable oil
¼ cup unsalted peanuts

For the sauce:

2 tablespoons light soy sauce
1 teaspoon wine vinegar
1 teaspoon sugar
1 teaspoon cornstarch
4 tablespoons water
salt and ground black pepper

Equipment

knife and chopping board
garlic press
grater
6 saucers
cup
measuring spoons
wok or large frying pan
wooden spoon

Stir-fried chicken with peanuts

1 Cut the chicken into small, bite-sized pieces. Trim the roots, tops, and outer leaves off the scallions and cut into slices.

2 Halve the pepper, pull out the core and seeds, then cut into thin slices.

3 Peel the garlic clove and crush in a garlic press. Peel the piece of ginger and grate it. Lay out all your dry ingredients on small saucers.

4 Mix all the sauce ingredients together in a cup and set aside.

5 Heat the oil in the wok or frying pan until very hot. Add the chicken pieces and stir well with the wooden spoon until they are brown and feel firm and cooked. This should take about 2 minutes.

Always be very careful when frying. Hot oil can be dangerous. Ask an adult to help you.

A taste of China

7 Now carefully pour in the sauce mixture, stirring well until it becomes thickened and glossy. Serve immediately with small bowls of plain, boiled rice.

6 Add the scallions, pepper, garlic, and ginger. Continue stirring and tossing for another 2 minutes. The vegetables should still be crisp but just lightly cooked. Mix in the peanuts.

Stir-fried chicken is a quick, delicious, and healthy meal.

Almond milk gelatin

This is a simple version of a Chinese dessert. Use soy milk, if you can find it. If you are a vegetarian, use agar-agar instead of gelatin.

1   Pour a little of the cold water into a small bowl. Sprinkle the gelatin over the water and stir lightly. Leave until the mixture turns solid and looks like wet sand.

2   Now stand the bowl in a saucepan of simmering water until the gelatin becomes a liquid.

Ingredients
Serves 4

1 packet of gelatin
1 cup milk
1 cup water
2–3 tablespoons sugar
1 teaspoon almond
   extract
7 oz. canned
   mandarin oranges
   or peaches in
   natural juice

Equipment

small bowl
2 saucepans
measuring cup
spoons
clean roasting pan,
   about 1 inch deep
chopping board
knife
can opener
4 small serving bowls

A taste of China

Always be very careful with hot liquid. Ask an adult to help you.

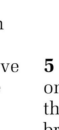

3 Put the rest of the water and the milk into a saucepan with the sugar and almond extract. Bring to a boil, remove from the heat, and stir in the gelatin.

5 Turn out the set gelatin onto a chopping board. To do this, dip the base of the pan briefly in hot water to loosen the bottom, and pull away the sides with your fingers.

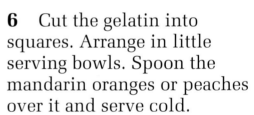

4 Allow to cool, then pour into a shallow, clean roasting pan. Put the pan into the refrigerator and allow to set until firm. This will take at least 3 hours.

6 Cut the gelatin into squares. Arrange in little serving bowls. Spoon the mandarin oranges or peaches over it and serve cold.

Glossary

Agar-agar A substance made from seaweed. It is used to make liquids gel.

Aromatic Having a strong, pleasant smell.

Bamboo A tall grass with hollow, woody stems. It can be used to make furniture and cooking equipment.

Barren Bare and unproductive. Barren land is not good for growing crops.

Braising A method of cooking food slowly in a little liquid.

Capital The main city of a country and the center of government.

Charcoal A fuel made from wood that has been partly burned to make black lumps.

Chopsticks A pair of sticks used in China and Japan for cooking and eating – as knives and forks are used in Western countries.

Civilization A society, or group of people, and the system of laws, farming, building, and the arts that they have developed.

Cleaver A heavy, ax-like knife with a large blade.

Climate The kind of weather a place generally has.

Community All the people who live in one place.

Continent One of the seven large areas of land that make up the world. They are Asia, Australia, Africa, Europe, North America, South America, and Antarctica.

Cuisine Style of cooking, usually from a certain region.

Curd A firm, creamy substance made from milk.

Dumplings Small balls of soft dough.

Dynasty A series of rulers from the same family. For many centuries, China was ruled by different dynasties.

Famines Severe shortages of food.

Fermented Made to ferment. Fermentation is a chemical change in food, usually caused by adding another substance, such as yeast.

Fertile Able to support a lot of plant growth. Fertile soil is good for growing crops.

Fertilizers Substances, such as manure, added to the soil to make it produce more crops.

Fuels Substances, such as coal, wood, or gas, that produce heat when burned.

Gelatin A substance made from animal bones. It is used to make liquids gel.

Graze To feed on the grass and other plants in a field.

Irrigation A system of watering the land using canals, ditches, and pumps.

Lotus The fruit of a water-lily that grows in tropical places.

Marinated Left to soak in a spicy liquid, usually made of spices, vinegar, and oil.

Millet A cereal crop grown for its edible grain.

Minority races Groups of people who differ in race from most of the rest of the people in a country.

Monsoon A wind in Asia that brings a season of heavy rain.

Noodles Ribbon-like strips of pasta (pasta is a paste or dough made of flour and water).

Nutrients Substances in the soil, such as minerals, that provide food for plants.

Paddies Fields flooded with water in which rice is grown.

Philosophy A system or school of thought.

Population The number of people living in a country.

Semi-tropical A word used to describe a certain type of weather. Tropical weather, found around the equator, is very hot and humid. Semi-tropical weather, found farther from the equator, is similar but less extreme.

Siberia A vast area of northern Asia, bordering the Arctic Circle. It is extremely cold.

Simmering Just below boiling.

Soy sauce A salty sauce made of fermented soybeans.

Spicy Containing lots of spices. Spices are aromatic substances, such as cinnamon.

State The government and all the people of a particular country.

Stock A liquid, full of flavor, made by boiling meat or fish bones, or vegetables, in water.

Toast To drink to someone's health and success.

Utensils Tools or equipment.

West, the The western part of the world which, through history, has been seen as different from eastern parts. Europe and America are part of the West.

Books to read

Information Books

China in Pictures.
Minneapolis: Lerner
Publications, 1989.

Kalman, Bobbie. *China—the
Culture.* New York: Crabtree
Publishing Co., 1989.

Lim, Jessie. *China.* North
Pomfret, VT: Trafalgar
Square, 1992.

Merton, D. and Yun-Kan,
Shio. *China: The Land and
Its People* (rev. ed.).
Morristown, NJ: Silver
Burdett Press, 1991.

Steele, Philip. *Journey
Through China.* Mahwah,
NJ: Troll Assoc., 1991.

Waterlow, Julia. *The Ancient
Chinese.* Look Into the Past.
New York: Thomson
Learning, 1994.

Recipe Books

Tan, Jennifer. *Food in China.*
Vero Beach, FL: Rourke
Corp., 1989.

Yu, Ling. *Cooking the Chinese
Way.* Minneapolis: Lerner
Publications, 1982.

Acknowledgments

The publishers would like to thank the following for allowing their photographs to be reproduced: Anthony Blake Photo Library 17, 20 top; Cephas 6 bottom (T. Stefanski), 10 top (N. Blythe); Eye Ubiquitous 8 top (J. Waterlow), 8 bottom right (P. Field), 9 top (F. Leather), 10 bottom (L. Fordyce), 11 both (J. Waterlow), 14 top (J. Waterlow), 15 both (J. Waterlow), 16 (J. Waterlow), 18 top (J. Waterlow), 18 bottom (J. Holmes), 20 bottom (J. Holmes), 21, 22 top (F. Leather), 24 top (B. Dean), 24 bottom (J. Holmes), 32 (P. Field); Hutchison Library 28 (R.-N. Giudicelli), 31 (T. Page); Panos Pictures *cover inset* (C. Platt), 12 (Wang Gang Feng), 13 bottom (A. le Garsmeur), 29 top (Wang Gang Feng), 30 top (A. le Garsmeur), 30 bottom (Wang Gang Feng); Tony Stone Worldwide *cover* (P. Long), 7 (H. Tse), 19 (J. Jackson); Julia Waterlow *frontispiece*, 4, 8 bottom left, 9 bottom, 22 bottom, 27, 33, 36, 38, 42; Wayland Picture Library 6 top (R. Sharpley), 13 top (J. Waterlow), 14 bottom (J. Waterlow), 23, 25 (J. Waterlow); Zefa 29 bottom.

The map artwork on page 5 was supplied by Peter Bull. The artwork on page 26 was supplied by John Yates. Recipe artwork on pages 34-35, 37, 39 and 41-44 was supplied by Judy Stevens.

The author would like to thank Deh-Ta-Hsiung for providing help and information.

Index